MY HEALTHY HABITS

REST
TO FEEL YOUR BEST

Norwood House Press

Madison Parker

Cataloging-in-Publication Data

Names: Parker, Madison.
Title: Rest to feel your best / Madison Parker.
Description: Buffalo, NY : Norwood House Press, 2026. | Series: My healthy habits | Includes glossary and index.
Identifiers: ISBN 9781978575370 (pbk.) | ISBN 9781978575387 (library bound) | ISBN 9781978575394 (ebook)
Subjects: LCSH: Rest--Juvenile literature. | Sleep--Juvenile literature.
Classification: LCC RA785.P375 2026 | DDC 612.76--dc23

Published in 2026 by
Norwood House Press
2544 Clinton Street
Buffalo, NY 14224

Designer: Rhea Magaro
Editor: Kim Thompson

Photo credits: Cover, p. 1 John_Walker_Shutter/Shutterstock.com; p. 5 Prostock studio/Shutterstock.com; p. 6 Art_Photo/Shutterstock.com; pp. 7, 10, 21 PeopleImages.com Yuri A/Shutterstock.com; p. 9 FREEPIK2/Shutterstock.com; p. 11 DimaBerlin/Shutterstock.com; p. 12 Kostenko Maxim/Shutterstock.com; p. 13 LightField Studios/Shutterstock.com; p. 14 Prostock studio/Shutterstock.com; p. 15 New Africa/Shutterstock.com; p. 16 Kenishirotie/Shutterstock.com; p. 17 Pixel Shot/Shutterstock.com; p. 18 Roman Samborskyi/ Shutterstock.com;

Printed in the United States of America

CPSIA compliance information: Batch #CSNHP26: For further information contact Norwood House Press at 1-800-237-9932.

TABLE OF CONTENTS

SLEEP IS IMPORTANT

Getting enough rest is an important part of staying healthy. When you sleep well, you feel **alert**. Your body and mind are able to grow, play, and learn.

STAYING ACTIVE DURING THE DAY

If you are **active** during the day, you will be ready for bed at night. Going to school and doing chores use up **energy**. Running and playing sports make your **muscles** work hard. At the end of a busy day, you feel tired.

Being outside during the day lets you soak up natural sunlight. When the sun goes down, your body will know it is time to rest.

LIMITING SCREEN TIME BEFORE BED

The light from TVs, tablets, and phones makes it harder to feel sleepy. Turn off screens at least an hour before bedtime. This will help you **relax**. It will tell your body that it is time for bed.

LISTENING TO YOUR BODY'S SLEEP SIGNALS

Yawning and rubbing your eyes are **signals** that your body needs rest. It is important to pay attention to these signs. They will help you get to bed before you feel too tired.

If you ignore these sleep signals, you may stay up too late. You may not get enough sleep. The next day, you might feel **grumpy** or have trouble focusing.

A BEDTIME ROUTINE

Start your bedtime **routine** at the same time every night. Your routine may include putting on pajamas, brushing your teeth, and washing your face.

Quiet activities, like reading a book or listening to soft music, can help you relax. Staying away from loud games or bright screens close to bedtime also helps you settle down.

A PLACE TO SLEEP

Being in a **cozy** space lets your body know it is time to rest. Get the room ready for sleep by turning off bright lights.

Close the curtains or blinds to make the room dark. Use a nightlight if you are afraid of the dark.

The **temperature** of the room is also important for a good night's sleep. A cooler room can help you feel more comfortable while you sleep.

A peaceful, quiet space helps you fall asleep quickly and stay asleep all night. Turn off anything that makes loud sounds. A fan can provide gentle background noise.

Get into a soft bed with warm blankets and a comfy pillow. That will make it easier to drift off to sleep.

RESTED AND HEALTHY

School-aged kids need 9 to 12 hours of sleep each night to feel well rested. Having a bedtime routine makes it easier to fall asleep and wake up ready to learn and play. Sleep gives your body the energy it needs to be healthy, stay active, and grow strong.

GLOSSARY

active (AK-tiv): busy and full of things to do

alert (uh-LURT): able to pay attention and take action

cozy (KOH-zee): warm, comfortable, and safe

energy (EN-ur-jee): the strength to do things without getting tired

grumpy (GRUHM-pee): cranky or in a bad mood

muscles (MUHS-uhlz): the parts of your body that allow you to move

relax (ri-LAKS): to slow down and become less stressed

routine (roo-TEEN): a series of actions that you do regularly; steps in a process

signals (SIG-nuhlz): signs that send a message or a warning

temperature (TEM-pur-uh-chur): how hot or cold something is

THINKING QUESTIONS

1. Why is it important to get enough sleep every night?

2. How many hours should kids sleep each night?

3. What are some ways to make a room cozy and comfortable for sleeping?

4. Why is it a good idea to turn off screens before bedtime?

5. What signals does your body give you when it's time to rest?

INDEX

ABOUT THE AUTHOR

Madison Parker spent her childhood in the city of Chicago, Illinois. A farm girl at heart, today she lives in Wisconsin with her husband and four children on a small farm with cows, goats, chickens, and two miniature horses named Harley and David. Her favorite dessert is vanilla frozen custard with rainbow sprinkles, even in the winter.